ABC in Chicago

ALL 'BOUT CITIES

Murray Hill Books LLC
www.murrayhillbooks.com

For Sophia,
Reading is the best
thing of all!

Robin Segal

Aa

aquarium

ambulances

Art
Institute

airport shuttle

Bb

Buckingham Fountain

bus stop

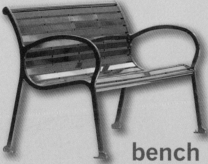

bench

basketball game

bus

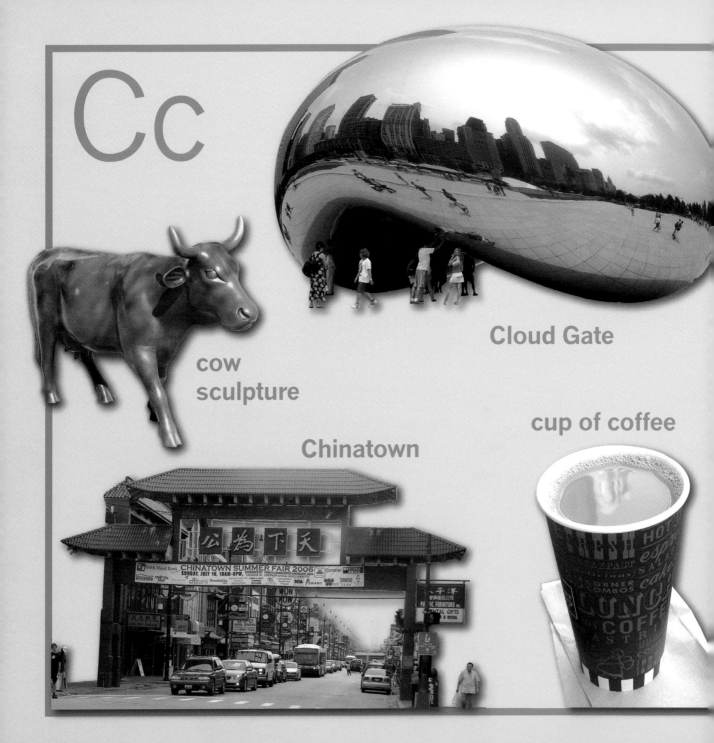

Cc

Cloud Gate

cow
sculpture

cup of coffee

Chinatown

cement
truck

clock

courier

Crown Fountain

Dd

dumpsters

deep dish pizza

dogs

deliveryman

drawbridge

Ee

escalator

elevated train

Ff

fire engine

Field Museum

ferris
wheel

flag

firefighters

flowers

Fine Arts
Building

Gg

garbage truck

geese

graffiti

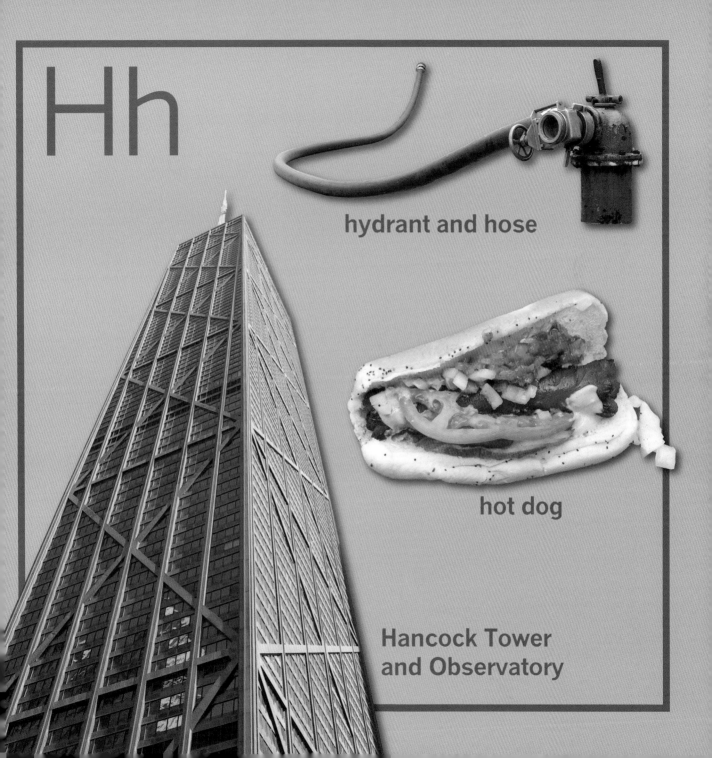

Hh

hydrant and hose

hot dog

Hancock Tower
and Observatory

Ii

Illinois
Institute
of
Technology

ice cream

Italian beef

Jj

juggler

joggers

jazz
funk
groove
band

Kk

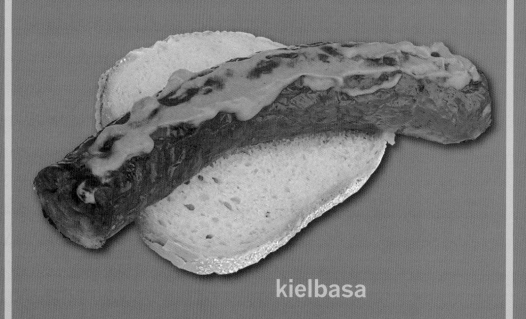

kielbasa

lamppost

LI

license plate

Lincoln Park

Lake Shore Drive

Lake Michigan

Mm

Michigan Avenue

**Marina
City**

map of Chicago

mural

manhole
covers

mailboxes

Merchandise
Mart

Nn

newspaper vending machines

North Avenue Beach

Navy Pier

Oo

overpasses

office
buildings

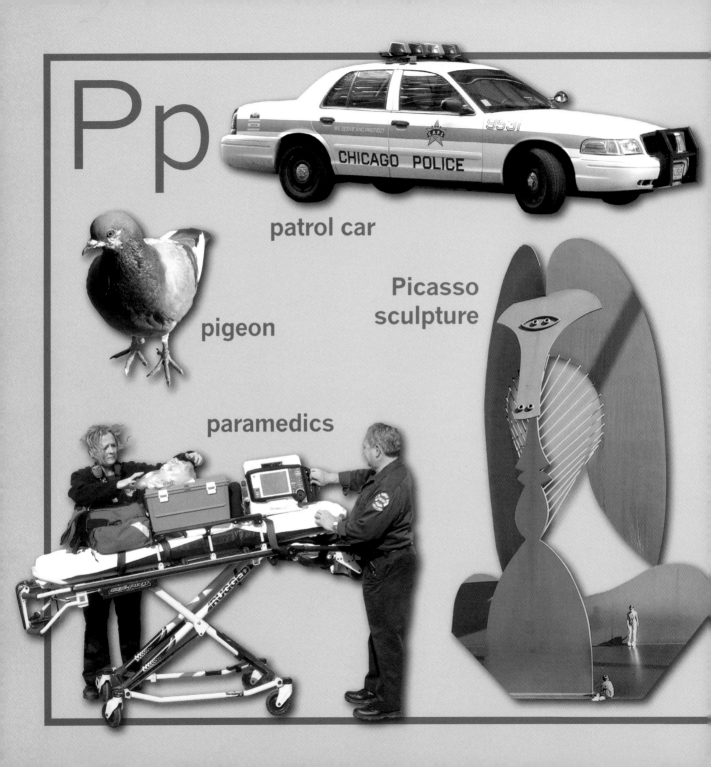

Pp

patrol car

pigeon

Picasso
sculpture

paramedics

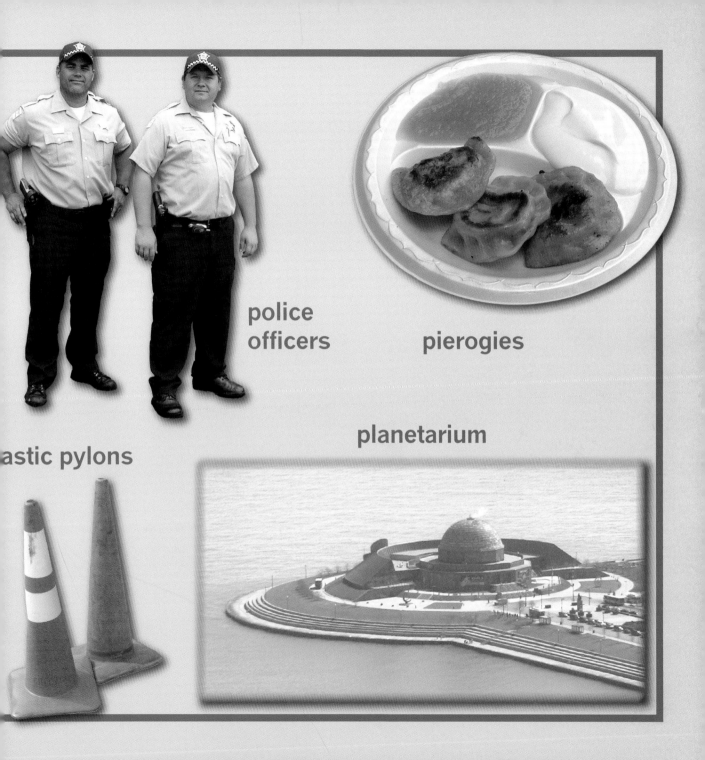

police
officers

pierogies

planetarium

astic pylons

Qq

Quigley Seminary

Rr

restrooms
sign

Reliance Building

rollerbladers

rose garden

Ss

steak

seagull

** HONORARY **
MIKE DITKA WAY

N RUSH ST

E CHESTNUT ST

street
signs

sculpture

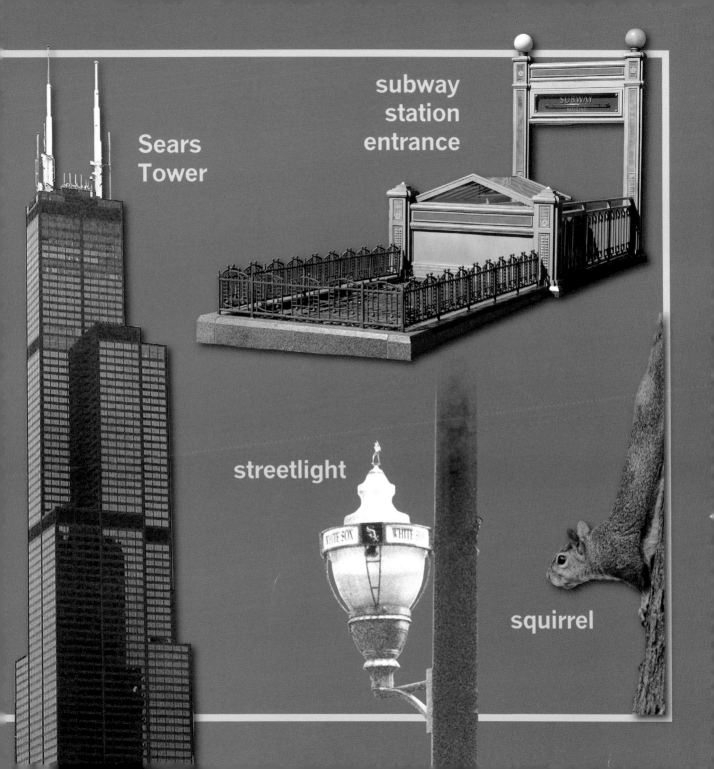

Sears
Tower

subway
station
entrance

streetlight

squirrel

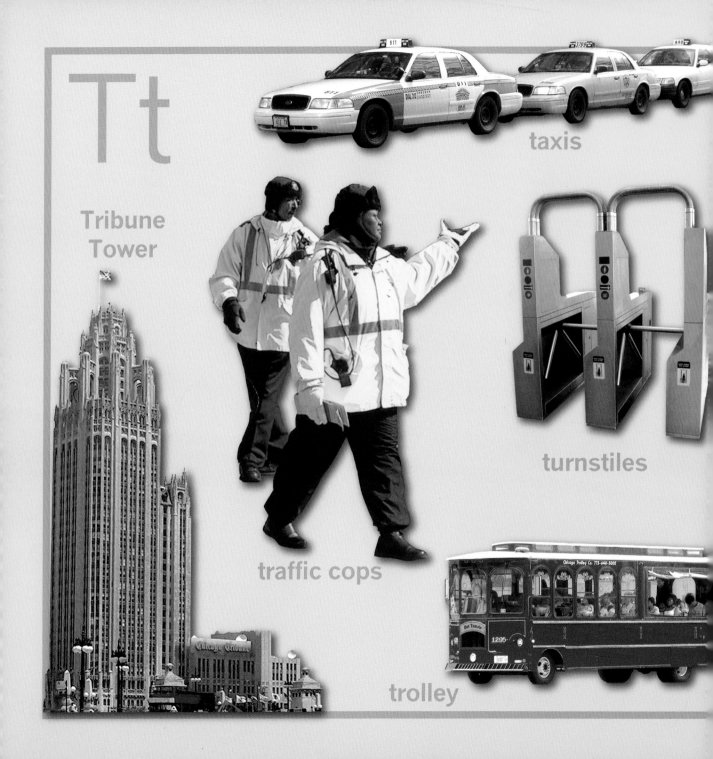

Tt

taxis

Tribune
Tower

turnstiles

traffic cops

trolley

Uu

trash
cans

umbrellas

University of Chicago

Vv

Victory Monument

volleyball game

walk signal

water fountain

Ww

window washer

Wrigley Building

Water Tower

WRIGLEY FIELD
HOME OF
CHICAGO CUBS

Wrigley Field

Xx

Xerox
Centre

Yy

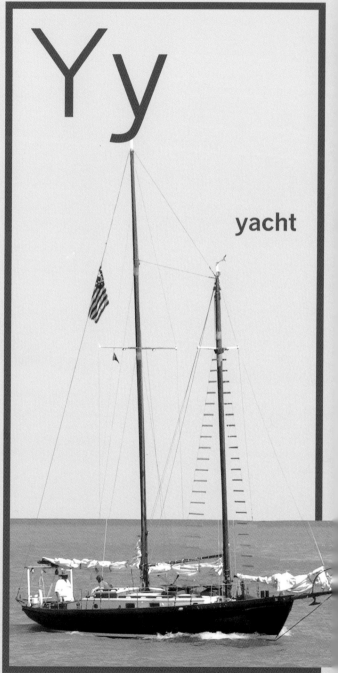

yacht

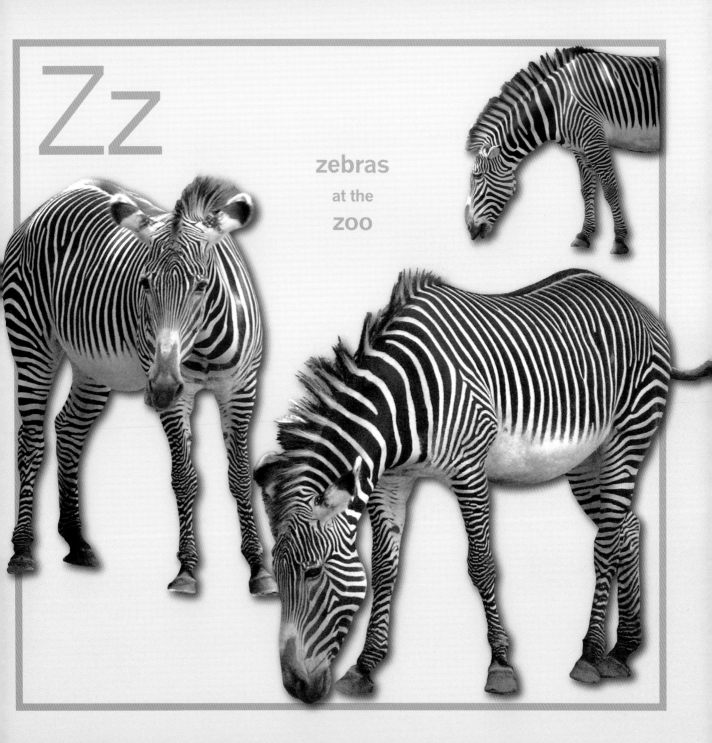

Zz

zebras
at the
ZOO

Murray Hill Books, LLC
P.O. Box 4393
New York, NY 10163

www.murrayhillbooks.com
info@murrayhillbooks.com
SAN 256-3622

Library of Congress Control Number: 2007924977
ISBN: 9780971969780

Photography, Design, and Editing by Robin Segal.
"All 'Bout Cities" is a Registered Trademark.

Look for more "All 'Bout Cities" titles at:

www.allboutcities.com